The EPIC Series

Text © Michael Brennan
Images © Catarina Neto

www.theepicseries.com

@theepicseriesofficial

For my wife, Kimberly, and the little one who made me a dad, Brayden.

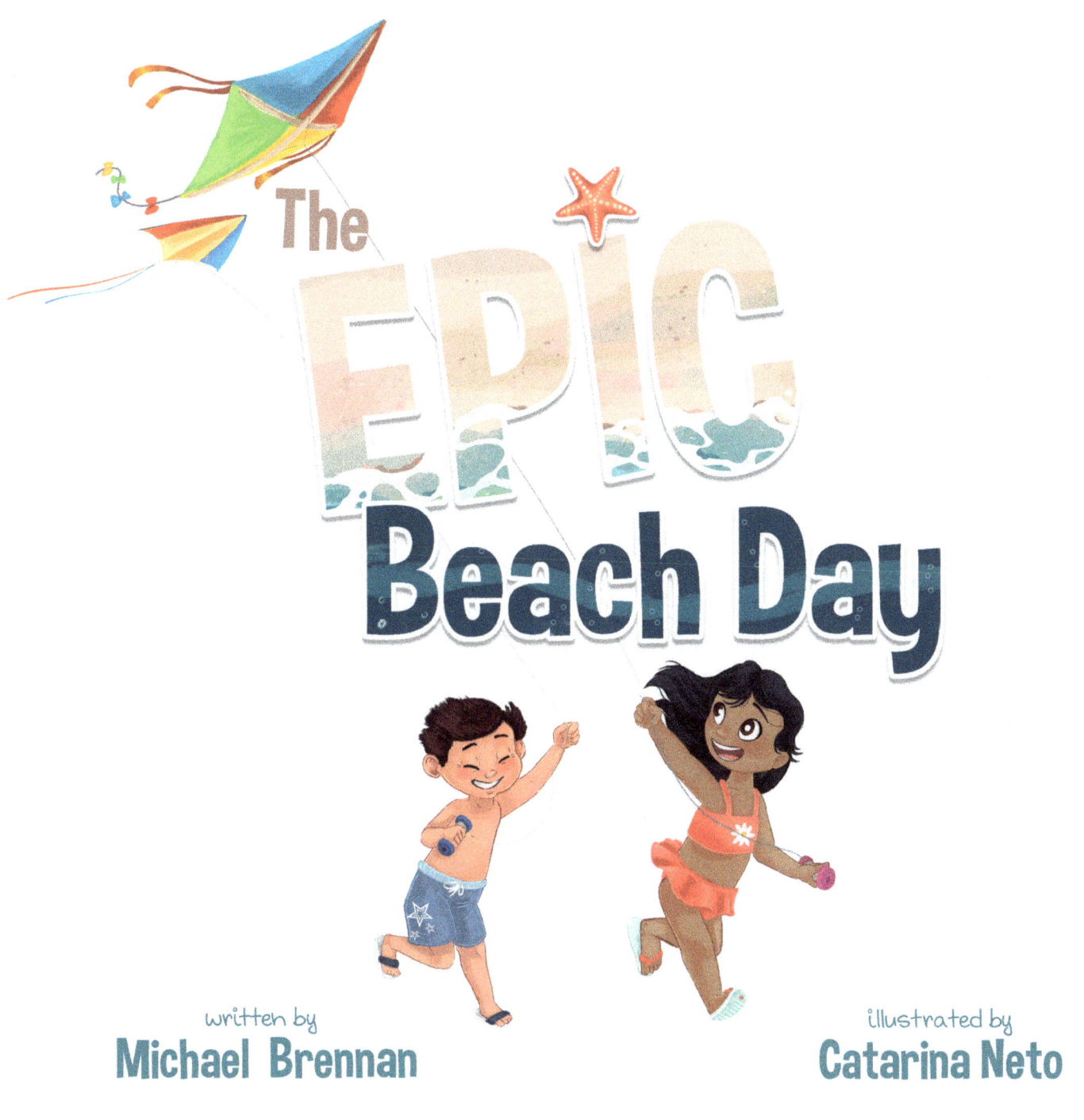

The EPIC Beach Day

written by
Michael Brennan

illustrated by
Catarina Neto

The morning sun rises,
Up over the dunes,
Reflects off the sea,
Waves crashing in tune.

Bikers and runners
Are starting their day.
The promenade's full.
Don't get in their way!

Down by the water,
There's yoga and stretching.
Some people have dogs;
It's frisbees they're fetching.

Here come the beachgoers,
Flocking in pairs,
Claiming their spots,
With umbrellas and chairs.

On-duty lifeguards
Sit on their stand.
They scope out the water
And place flags in the sand.

Surfers catch waves
Both powerful and tall.
They could stay in forever
And ride them all.

Kids play with beach balls
And dump out their toys.
Many buckets and shovels
For the girls and the boys.

Out in the distance,
You can see dolphins' fins
Coming up to the surface
Then dipping back in.

Fishermen cast lines
Out past the jetty.
If they reel in a fish,
They'll have the net ready!

No sharks in the water
So, swimmers take laps.
Soon to get tired,
And have to take naps.

Parents lay out
For a chance to get tan.
Now they have sunburn.
That wasn't the plan!

Kids stop for lunch,
After building sand castles.
The seagulls drop in,
And cause a big hassle!

The ice cream man strolls,
With his cooler of sweets.
He yells "fudgy wudgy"
As kids run from their seats.

Along the shoreline,
As the water recedes,
Clams and crabs dig,
Hiding under seaweed.

It's almost low tide,
Waves head out to sea,
Exposing more seashells
For you and for me.

The breeze picks up,
And the clouds roll by.
Kids run upwind,
Flying kites in the sky.

It's time to pack up
And start heading back.
A short walk to the house
To grab a quick snack.

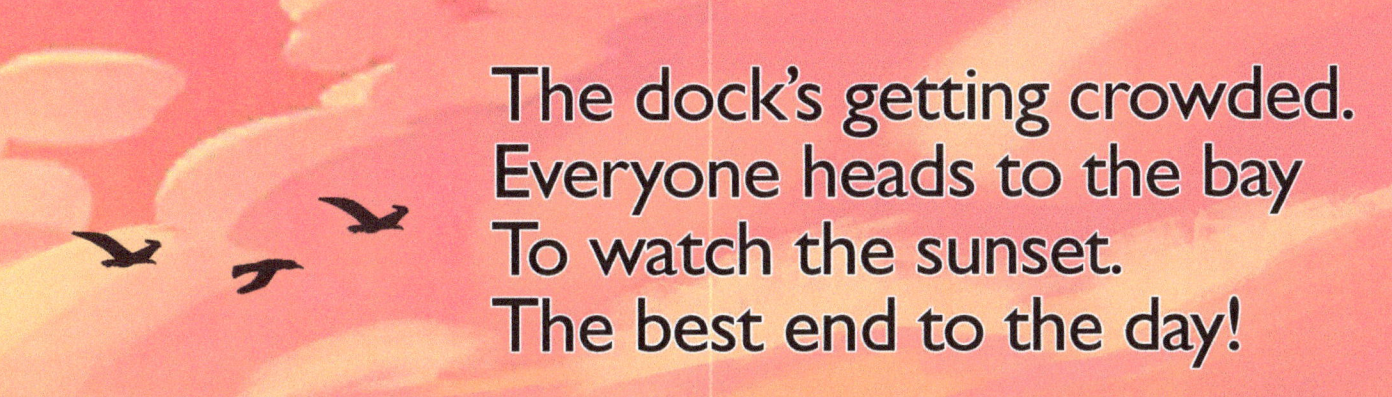

The dock's getting crowded.
Everyone heads to the bay
To watch the sunset.
The best end to the day!

Overview & About The Author

The Epic Beach Day is the first book in "the epic series" by Michael Brennan and is a children's book that was inspired by Mike's annual family vacations to Sea Isle City, NJ. He seeks to highlight the beauty in the routine beach day, push back against the distractions of screens and technology, and embrace the presence of family, friends, and loved ones around us. He hopes this book will encourage children to experience the beauty in nature, learn and grow through their peers, and be fully present in the moment. The book aims to spark curiosity, inspire adventure, and motivate kids to create their own life long memories. Mike currently resides in Bucks County, Pennsylvania, with his beautiful wife, Kimberly, and their son, Brayden. His hobbies include traveling, soccer, pickleball, skiing, and enjoying family walks.

Acknowledgments

I wanted to start by thanking my wife, Kim, for believing that I could turn this idea into a finished product as well as supporting me through the entire process. You are the best!

Thanks to my dad who did everything possible to ensure I had the best childhood and was surrounded by the family and support system that I needed growing up. I love you!

Thanks Nana, Pop-pop, and the entire Brennan family for the endless fun and games on our family vacations. From digging holes to drippy castles, running the bases to foursquare, and so many other games we created from scratch, it helped spark my creative side. When the day was over and none of us wanted to leave, cleaning up to come home from the beach, and making family dinners taught me the importance of teamwork and responsibility, all while creating core memories. I love you all!

Thank you, Gam, Pop, and the entire Grimaldi family, for hosting sleepovers at the Villas, Sea Isle along the promenade, and countless summers spent at Aunt Linda's and Uncle Chris'. Playing card games in the Florida room, crabbing on the bridge, and searching for horseshoe crabs at the bay were some of my favorite memories and I will forever cherish those times. I love you guys!

Huge thank you to my cousin Christie for editing my work and big thanks to my cousin Sean, Kim's cousin Jess, and my aunt Michelle for giving me honest feedback, encouraging me to finish what I started, and providing advice, information, and resources. It was all extremely helpful!

Thank you to my illustrator Catarina. You brought my vision to life and I am forever thankful that I found you. You are a great communicator, pay close attention to detail, and take great pride in your final product. I look forward to working with you on future books!